El Bordo Journo!

Fifteen years as a border journalist in
San Diego-Tijuana

P. J. SÁINZ

ISBN-13: 978-1537403540
ISBN-10: 1537403540

"And whatsoever ye do, do it heartily,
as to the Lord, and not unto men."
Colossians 3:23

Frontera,
frontera internacional:
abre que voy a pasar
Los Tigres del Norte

All praise, and honor, and glory be to God, Jesus Christ, King of Kings, and Lord of Lords.

I dedicate this book, fruit of my 15 years as a journalist, to my dear wife and best friend, Eliud, ·
and to the heritage Our Lord has given us,
our beautiful children,
Dafne and Bruno.

Fifteen years telling stories about the border

I could've been a journalist in Los Angeles, where I grew up.

But after visiting the border, I saw the potential of stories I could tell being a journalist in the San Diego-Tijuana region. That's when I decided to stay.

It's been 15 years: It was in September, 2001, a few days before the terrorist attacks that changed our nation, when I formally started my career as a journalist, no longer as a student journalist, but as a formal journalist out in the streets, making a living for himself and his wife.

This September marked a decade and a half since I became a reporter in the San Diego-Tijuana border region, with a special emphasis on arts and culture, on the stories of common people living in this corner of the world.

I arrived in San Diego in January 2000, after transferring to the journalism program at San Diego State University, after living for almost three years in Santa Barbara, where I didn't see myself as a professional journalist.

Before that I lived my late childhood and all of my adolescence in Huntington Park, one of the cities with one of the highest concentrations of Mexican immigrants in Los Angeles.

And even before that, I was born and I lived my first years in Navolato, a small city in the northern Mexican state of Sinaloa, where the weather is very hot.

Since I was a kid I decided to become a journalist -- or rather, a writer. You see, in Navolato, as a good Sinaloan city, the news goes from mouth to mouth. People, let's say, has a good eye to see the speck in other people's eye, and a fine ear and a lose tongue to tell everything. So, from an early age I was interested in listening to people tell stories (some real, some fake, some in between).

In L.A., writing helped me to save the memories I had of Navolato, that city I missed so much during my teenage years (especially my beloved Eliud, my childhood best friend who is now my dear wife).

Thanks to Heavenly Father I was able to put to good use that talent to tell stories I got from my Sinaloan ancestors: Not as gossip, but as useful, trustworthy information that can help readers improve their lives.

The pages in this book are a testimony that God has blessed me, without me deserving it.

In 15 years, I've been able to make a living for my family writing, telling real stories from the border, interviewing from famous singers and artists to people in the streets and me.

Being a border journalist is a blessing from Jesus Christ, my Lord and my God.

My Tortured Relationship With Journalism

"¡El Debate de Culiacán!" I would hear as the Volkswagen Beetle passed in front of my house in my native city of Navolato, in the northern Mexican state of Sinaloa, every morning while I was getting ready for elementary school.

A loud voice from the speakers on top of the car would shout out the day's headlines, trying to persuade people to come out and buy the paper: "¡Y andale! ¡Compre su periodico, El Debate de Culiacán!"

Before leaving for school, while eating breakfast at the table, I would read the comics: *Condorito*, *Snoopy*, and *Daniel el Travieso*. They always made me laugh. But I wasn't the only one with a newspaper, it was definitely a family affair: My great-grandfather, Tata Pablito, would buy *Noroeste* daily.

Growing up in Sinaloa, my first encounter with journalism was in Spanish. From the pages of El Debate to the wrinkled face of Jacobo Zabludovsky in *24 Horas*, I was always surrounded by news. But this news, I would later learn, was extremely censored by the government. The few courageous journalists who dared to criticize the government or the narcos (Sadly, Sinaloa is home to the most powerful drug cartels in Mexico) in their writings were brutally executed.

I was barely in elementary school, but I was already aware of the political and economic problems in Mexico. And *periodismo*, it was said in Sinaloa, wasn't a glamorous career to pursue. In Mexico, freedom of the press was, and to some point, still is, just a myth.

The same government that filled my childhood newspapers with lies, forced my family and me to immigrate to the United States in 1990. I was 11.

Since I had attended a Catholic elementary school where English was taught and I was a fanatic of American cinema, I already had a command of the English language when I arrived in Los Angeles. My second encounter with journalism took place.   But now, instead of Spanish, the news was written in English; instead of lies, truth. Here in the United States I still found a problem with journalism, though. In Mexico I was always part of the majority. It wasn't difficult for me to relate to the shows on television or the stories in newspapers. In the United States I became part of a minority, and that minority, I began to notice, wasn't on the front page of the newspaper nor on my television's screen.

Both of my encounters with journalism, in Spanish and in English, in Mexico and in the United States, had been shadowed by censorship and discrimination. I knew I had to do something.

Today I'm a long way from Sinaloa. I've been a professional journalist in the San Diego and Tijuana border region for 15 years.   I chose this career to finally repair the tortured relationship between journalism and I: No more censorship; no more discrimination.

I write about important forgotten issues. I thank my Lord Jesus Christ I am blessed to share stories which otherwise may never be told.

'We're letting the world know we are here'

In 1970, when Chicano activists took over the grounds of what today is known as Chicano Park, Ramón "Chunky" Sánchez was there, strumming songs on his guitar. Now, 37 years later, Sánchez is tuning his guitar once more to support the Mexican and Mexican-American community in San Diego at this iconic Barrio Logan park.

"The guitar has always been the weapon of the movement," said Sánchez, singer of the local combo Los Alacranes (the Scorpions).

Saturday marks the 37th anniversary of the taking of Chicano Park. The annual Chicano Park Day celebration this year will revolve around the central theme "We didn't cross the border, the border crossed us," referring to the territory ceded by Mexico to the United States more than 150 years ago, lands that included California.

"We're letting the world know we are here," said Tommie Camarillo, president of the Chicano Park Steering Committee, who's in charge of Chicano Park Day and the daily administration of the park.

Sánchez will play songs like "El primero de mayo" ("The First of May"), which recalls the immigration boycotts and marches from last year.

"I've always played music for immigrants," he said. "Los Alacranes play music for the people."

The subject of undocumented immigration and the discrimination faced by undocumented immigrants in the United States has been a powerful source of inspiration for many singers.   Immigration issues will assume a central role at Saturday's event, Camarillo said, referring to immigration raids carried out by federal agents in recent weeks at homes and workplaces in San Diego and other parts of the country.

"People are tired of this," she said.

Salvador Barajas, one of Chicano Park's original muralists and the person who every year designs the official poster of the celebration, said he chose the subject of immigration to underscore the pain caused by the raids.

"It's important we're conscious of what's going on," he said. "It's our way of supporting the end of these raids."

This year's special guest is Enrique Morones, one of San Diego's most prominent activists in support of immigrants' rights. He will give a speech in which he will pay homage to the more than 4,000 people who have died while trying to cross the border.

"The subject of immigration has never been more important," he said. "I want to make it personal with real stories. There are more than 4,000 stories."

But the activist, who founded the pro-immigrant Border Angels group, said it is necessary for Latinos to raise their voices in order to stop discrimination against the undocumented, most of whom are Mexican.

"We can all participate in the discourse," he said. "We can all pick up the telephone and tell our legislators: 'We want a dignified and humane immigration reform for the 12 million undocumented immigrants in this country, we want a humane way of entering the country.'"

Morones said he has proposed a memorial monument to the people who have died along the border since 1994, when Operation Gatekeeper was launched. Camarillo said Chicano Park's executive committee voted and approved Morones' idea. Right now, a group of artists that includes Barajas is planning the proposal that will be presented to the committee.

According to Camarillo, the word "border" has many meanings in Chicano Park. She said it could refer to the many obstacles faced by Mexicans in San Diego: discrimination, the lack of basic services, racism.

"Coronado Bridge (under which the park is located) is the great wall of Barrio Logan," she said.

Besides celebrating one more year since the park's founding, the community will also celebrate the summer start of restoration work on Chicano Park's murals, thanks to the $1.6 million grant the park committee received from the state.

"Chicano Park is the heart of the movement in San Diego," said Morones. The celebration will include, besides the pro-immigrant speeches, music, food, poetry and dance.

And, of course, Sánchez's guitar will be there.

"Change can't happen in our community without artists, without poets, without musicians," he said. "They inspire the people's mood. They give hope."

(2007)

Work by young visual journalists shows 'another world'

Luis Abel Ramírez, 11, already knows what he wants to be when he grows up: a journalist.

When he was behind the camera, they loaned him to take pictures of his neighborhood, *colonia* Fausto González, one of the poorest in the city, Luis Abel says, he felt a rush of excitement when he captured images and shared them.

One of his photographs shows a group of children in front of a trash-strewn hill. Another shows a man dismantling a car, possibly stolen. Yet another shows his grandmother sitting, surrounded by her grandchildren.

"I was out on the street, going everywhere with my camera, and I liked it a lot," a smiling Luis Abel says. "People even told me I looked like a reporter."

Some 40 photographs taken by Luis Abel, his sister Elvira and four of their cousins will be part of "Children of the Dump: Photographs by the Children of Tijuana's Municipal Dump," which runs through the end of the month at The Front, the cultural center run by Casa Familiar in San Ysidro.

The show, which made a stop at a Tijuana gallery recently, is part of "The Tijuana Project," a documentary that independent filmmaker John Sheedy has been shooting for almost two years about the children of the *colonia* Fausto González, site of the city's old municipal dump.

It was the children themselves who showed an interest in using still cameras, Sheedy says, proof that poverty is no enemy to creativity and talent.

"The children asked us if they could borrow the cameras for a while, to take pictures of their families and friends," he says.

The six children kept the cameras for a year, taking hundreds and hundreds of pictures of everyday life in the *colonia*.

The experience of taking their own photographs was a ray of hope for these kids, who live in makeshift houses of cardboard, metal sheets and bits of lumber, says Sheedy, who lives in Durango, Colo., and comes to Tijuana every month to work on the documentary.

"When you grow up next to an old dump and your parents make their living by going through the trash, looking for things to sell, the future doesn't seem very promising," he says. "For these children, art, photography, really is something that will help set goals outside the dump."

José Adán Ramírez, Luis Abel's cousin, says the ideas for his pictures would just come to him.

"I'd be walking down the street and all of a sudden I'd want to take pictures of the houses, of the other kids," says José Adán, 11, nicknamed "El Chapo," or Shorty.

This month, Eve Tulbert, a young woman from Los Angeles who came to work as a volunteer to plan the exhibition alongside freelance photographer David Maung, held an informal session where the children came up with titles for each of the 40 pictures in the show.

One of the photographs, which shows a boy making local gang signs, was titled "El Cholito" (The little cholo). Another photograph, of a group of children playing on top of an old tire made into a swing, is called "Un lugar especial" (A special place).

Mónica Hernández, director of art and culture at San Ysidro's The Front, said the photo exposition is a way to show San Diego County residents the reality of living in Tijuana's poorest neighborhoods.

"It's important that people in San Diego know there exists another world in the *colonias* near the old town dump," Hernández says. "It's something that needs to be discussed more to see how we can help."

The municipal dump at the *colonia* Fausto González ceased operation two years ago, leaving many of these children's relatives out of a job. The city relocated the dump to a site next to the free road to Tecate.

"They closed the dump some three months after I began filming the documentary, and these children's lives changed forever," Sheedy says. "The families send the children to a school in the *colonia*, and the parents go to work at the new dump near Tecate almost every day."

Besides photography, the children have also been involved in theater, writing and arts workshops, thanks to funds provided by foundations that support Sheedy's work in Tijuana.

The photographs will be on sale to create a scholarship program for the children in the documentary, which will be finished in early 2009.

The children say their dream is to have their own cameras.

"This is a unique story in a place that's usually very depressing," the filmmaker says. "These photographs are a celebration of this community."

(2008)

'The past and present are there'

Chicano Park's murals are the history textbooks of *la raza*, the informal means of communication among Mexicans, the monument to the past struggles of Chicanos in San Diego.

The almost 70 murals in the park are a testimony to events in the history of the United States, of Mexico and of the Chicano community, but above all, these murals emphasize the culture that residents of Mexican descent have forged in Barrio Logan, the heart of Mexican culture in San Diego.

On the park's walls are represented such Mexican heroes as Benito Juárez, César Chávez, Frida Kahlo and the Virgin of Guadalupe. They also tell the story of the founding of Tenochtitlán and of the Mexican Revolution.

Other murals depict more recent events, including the takeover of the park by Barrio Logan's residents on April 22, 1970.

"The past and present are there," says Salvador Barajas, one of the park's original muralists who, every year, designs the poster for Chicano Park Day, celebrating its 38th anniversary on Saturday.   The theme of this year's celebration is "Our Lives, Culture and History As Seen Through Our Murals," says Víctor Ochoa, an artist involved with the planning and execution of Chicano Park's murals.

"There is no censorship there. The murals are like weapons, tools, to help find a solution to the problems that our people face," he said.

The murals say "no" to racism, discrimination and sexism, he added, and "yes" to human rights, diversity and to being proud of Mexican heritage.

"Instead of books, we paint murals," said muralist Mario Torero. "It's the immediate publishing of history."

Because historical events, and current issues like immigration, are depicted from a Chicano point of view, people who disagree with that viewpoint have damaged the murals many times. Vandals have covered the murals with graffiti, thrown paint on them and even shot at them.

In 1979, Ochoa said, a group of people wearing the white robes of the Klu Klux Klan and carrying signs that read "White Power" launched paint bombs at the murals. Also, time and the elements have damaged them bit-by-bit. Many of the murals were painted "guerrilla style" during the struggle to save the park, and archival techniques were not used.

"I'm a little bit surprised they're still there after being so ill-treated," said Barajas.

In 2002, Caltrans, the agency in charge of maintenance for the Coronado Bridge, under which the park sits, and the Chicano Park Steering Committee, the community group that manages the park and organizes Chicano Park Day, received $1.6 million in federal funds to restore some of the most extensively damaged murals. But regulations and red tape in Sacramento have so far kept the funds from being used.

"The process has been very slow, almost painfully so for those who have been most closely involved," says Martin Rosen, environmental planner and cultural representative for Caltrans.   "No one imagined the process would take so long."
Rosen, who originally requested the funds in 1999, says Caltrans will begin a search for a restoration project director in a couple of months. He says the agency expects the renovation work to start in six months or so.

Caltrans and the Chicano Park Steering Committee published a technical manual, in which Barajas and Ochoa recommend how to make the restoration project a success. "We've been very patient for the project to start," said Ochoa.

Many of the artists who painted the murals were anonymous, others are elderly now, others are dead. This year's Chicano Park Day Celebration is an homage to the artists who left their mark on the park.

Without the murals, recognized worldwide for their cultural and historical value, Chicano Park wouldn't be the same, Ochoa said.

"The murals rescue the historic part that makes the park a spiritual place, not just a concrete jungle beneath the Coronado Bridge."

(2008)

Kids' chess booms unchecked

We are in a house in the Colonia Mariano Matamoros, in the La Presa district, one of the poorest in the city. There are discarded tires in front of the house. A polluted stream runs along one side. The street is not paved. Dogs meander around.

Inside the home, however, the five Aceves siblings don't care what happens around them as long as they're playing what they love most: chess.

Their father, Alfredo Aceves, knows that when he dies, he won't be able to leave his five children many material possessions. But he also knows that he was able to teach them to play the game.

"Chess makes children think; it makes them plan their strategies to win," says Aceves, a 45-year-old taxi driver in Chula Vista. "They have to think five or six moves ahead before making them. That's exactly what life is about: preparing yourself, planning things well, making the best decision."

The Aceves children, from 9 to 16 years old, are an example of the boom chess is having in Tijuana, especially among lower-and middle-class youngsters.

So much so, in fact, that chess is one of the most popular categories in the championships organized by the municipal sports department. The players, who, like the Aceves kids, range in age from 9 to 16, will receive medals, diplomas and T-shirts.

The municipal chess final, which will pit the best player of each district or *delegación*, is Saturday at the department's facilities.

Of the 250 participants in the tourney, the bulk come from the La Presa and Sanchez Taboada districts, among the city's poorest.

"We're surprised," says Eliseo Sandoval, the agency's director of the popular sports department. "The stereotype is that only people from wealthier backgrounds play this sport. Here we're proving this isn't so."

During the current city administration, the department has stepped up efforts to reach poorer communities. It has hired promoters to travel to these parts to encourage greater participation in sports, chess among them.

"More than promoters, they're missionaries," a smiling Sandoval says.

It's in these areas that sports facilities, like basketball courts and community gyms, are covered by graffiti or abandoned.

"These are the children who are at greatest risk," Sandoval says. "Until now, they hadn't been taken into account because they lived so far from the city center. Those children never come (to the department), because they don't even have bus fare."

The five official sports played in Tijuana schools are soccer, basketball, volleyball, track and field and, to the surprise of many, chess.

"Chess had never received this much importance," Sandoval says.

More and more middle and high schools in Tijuana are establishing chess clubs. Usually, when a youngster learns to play, he or she teaches his classmates.

Little by little, school chess teams are forming, says Juan José Gómez, president of the Baja California Association of Chess Players, whose mission is "to promote and defend chess."

The association has 350 active members in 10 chapters around the state. About 60 percent are under age 20.

"Young people are attracted to it because of the depth of the game, because it's a challenge, because it makes them think." he said. "And, no matter how much you practice, you never stop learning. There are always ways to get better at the game. They never get bored."

In fact, the association plans to open its first chess school next month.

For the Aceves children, any place is a good place to play chess, even atop two of the beds in the two-bedroom home where they live.

Six years ago, thanks to a fellow cabdriver, their father learned to play chess.

"I used to like playing cards and Chinese checkers, but chess always interested me. When I learned that this co-worker played, I asked him to teach me. Little by little, I began to understand the rules."

That was when he decided to teach his oldest son, Alfredo Jr., now 16, to play the game. He went on to become a chess champion at his high school – and a celebrity among his classmates.

"First I taught him," says the dad, smiling. "And then I was never able to beat him again.

"For me it's very important that they learn chess, because it keeps them busy doing something positive. They are very active; they're always running or playing at something. Chess makes them focus their energy on something positive."

His wife, Enedina Ruiz, agrees.

"I see them settled down while they play. That's when I get the chance to cook dinner or do housework."

The other Aceves children – Enedina, 12; Miguel, 11; Jesús, 10; and Maria Guadalupe, 9 – are also preparing for the municipal tournament. To do this, they play one or two games every day.

"It makes me very proud seeing a family like this," says Sandoval, of the sports department. "This gentleman didn't wait for the government to offer his children something better; instead, he took the reins himself."

It doesn't matter if his children win or lose in the tourney, the dad says. As a reward for having participated, he plans to take them to a taco dinner.

(2006)

Girl Scouts cherish their bilingual troop

Ten-year-old Génesis Luévano prefers to do outdoor activities with other girls than spend her afternoons after school watching TV.

"That way I'm not cooped up for so long," said Génesis, who, along with her four sisters, are part of a Girl Scout troop in this community.

Activities outside the home, even modest ones, can mean a lot to girls growing up in a community like this one, with few resources.

"What they learn in Girl Scouts isn't taught in school," said Irene Barajas, a 53-year-old businesswoman.

In the 1980s, she founded the first bilingual Girl Scout troop in San Ysidro for Latina girls so they could have opportunities that were not only fun but educational.

Then she moved away, to the Mexican state of Chihuahua, where she lived for several years.

She returned four years ago and restarted the Girl Scout troop, the county's only bilingual one and, with almost 50 girls, its largest.

The group grew a bit larger one Saturday last month, when eight more girls officially joined.

"Welcome to Troop 5912!" Barajas shouted to the new girls after the initiation ceremony, held in the backyard of her San Ysidro home.

"Today you make a promise to serve God, your country and your fellow humans. You are going to become part of something very special. Doors will open to a new world, but one which has responsibilities."

That afternoon, the girls made Christmas ornaments that later were shared with the residents of the Windsor Gardens Convalescent Center in National City.

The Girl Scouts organization, founded in 1912, has stepped up efforts to recruit more Latinas in recent years.

Barajas said that when she started her first troop, Girl Scouts had no information in Spanish.

"At the events, you would only see Anglo girls," she said. "Mine were the only Latinas."

That's changed.

Girl Scouts of San Diego has packets in Spanish for Latino parents, and the Web site includes information in that language as well.

All this is meant to increase the troops' diversity, said Desiree Nash, director of community development for the Girl Scouts of San Diego and Imperial counties, which have a total 2,200 troops with 28,000 girls.

The girls and their parents feel at home at the San Ysidro troop.

"Should I tell you in English or Spanish?" Barajas asked some girls before instructing them on how to make Christmas ornaments.

"Irene understood the value and the experience that the Girl Scouts would give to girls who don't have many opportunities to explore beyond their communities," Nash said. "Irene and her co-leaders are helping to forge girls with courage, self-confidence and character, who will make the world a better place."

But the troop leader said it hasn't been easy getting Latina mothers to understand the benefits that come from being part of the Girl Scouts.

Cultural differences and economic challenges made it difficult for the troop to grow.

"Mexican moms won't hand over their girls until there is a sense of trust. At the beginning, when we went to an event, there would be 14 girls accompanied by 10 moms," Barajas said.

Now, more mothers are willing to let their daughters attend troop events by themselves.

A majority of the girls come from homes headed solely by the mother, some of whom work two jobs to make ends meet.

"They see very little of their daughters. Some tell me, 'Sign them up for everything,'" Barajas said.

While girls in other troops can sell up to 2,000 boxes of cookies, one of the most traditional of Girls Scout activities, Barajas said the most a San Ysidro girl has ever sold is 50 boxes.

"These girls really have a hard time selling cookies. People struggle to support their own kids," she added. "When you have to count every dollar to get ahead, you're not going to spend $4 on a box of cookies when at the 99 cent store you can buy a big box for $1."

The girls in Troop 5912 said Girls Scouts have helped them cope and at times overcome the challenges they face in their daily lives. Itzel Barrón, 12, joined the troop three years ago. Since then, she said, her schoolwork and home life have improved.

"It's helped me to set goals," she said.

María Flores is one of the mothers who at first didn't know too much about the Girl Scouts. But now, almost one year after her daughter Ambar joined, the mom sees the benefits.

"It's helped her to get along with other girls and at the same time respect the rules more," she said.

Delma Andrade knows firsthand the impact the organization can have on a girl. She was a member of the 1980s troop.

When she found out Barajas was restarting the troop, Andrade didn't hesitate a minute to join her. At age 29, she's now one of the assistant leaders and helps others the way she had been helped.

"The Girl Scouts was our escape," Andrade said. "It helped me to focus. It was something very positive."

Eight-year-old Jodie Astrop says she likes going to new places and learning new things with her fellow troop members. There's one thing she likes above all:

"I have a lot of friends."

(2006)

Poor but proud *El Maclovio* fights the odds

Jacqueline Hernández was 10 years old when her family arrived in a place in the middle of nowhere that today is the community of Maclovio Rojas.

She remembers how the area was a deserted, dusty spot some 10 miles from Tijuana on the free road to Tecate.

There were no modern housing developments nearby nor large assembly plants where many of Maclovio's residents work.

The Hernández family was one of 25 that founded the community in April 1988, and even though she was just a girl, she remembers the obstacles they faced to settle there.

The families were made up of farmers, many of them Mixteco Indians from the southern state of Oaxaca who were searching for a place to live. They settled on land no one else wanted.

They named their community after Maclovio Rojas, a Mixteco leader who had been fatally struck by a car in the San Quintin Valley in 1987.

"We have achieved much since then," Hernández says.

The residents have opened two elementary schools and one middle school, a trade school and a Casa de la Mujer, where the women receive social services.

They also have developed a vibrant micro-economy thanks to the small businesses that sprang up along the road and the mobile carts that sell all types of wares.

Hernández continues to live at Maclovio, one of the isolated, poor colonias east of the city. Just as she did, her two sons are growing up there.

She says she's proud of the advances the *Maclovianos* have made in their community, despite lacking such basic services as power and drinking water.

She works as the administrator of the Aguascalientes Community Center, where the residents hold meetings and organize social and cultural events.

Murals painted on the center's walls tell the settlement's history, and the challenges its families faced to get ahead.

An estimated 2,500 families live there now, some 12,000 inhabitants.

Those who can afford them live in brick houses. Those with less, build their houses of laminate, wood and even cardboard.

As the settlement begins its 20th year, its residents continue to wage a battle to obtain title to their land, which, in the eyes of the law, belongs to the Ejido Francisco Villa, a neighboring farm cooperative.

In recent weeks, in fact, representatives of the residents' association have staged a hunger strike and a sit-in at the state government building in Tijuana, demanding better services for Maclovio.

Since the residents do not have the necessary documents, the federal and state governments consider the settlement to be illegal.   That's why state officials can't take drinking water there, even though the water company's central plant is located beside Maclovio.

Jesús Octavio Montaño, a Baja California official, says the distribution of farmland is the federal government's job and that the state has no jurisdiction to issue land titles.

Yet, he says, "It's urgent that the Maclovio Rojas families be served."

In fact, the state government has started to help. It pays the teachers' salaries and supervised and validated the schools' academic plan.

Even so, resources are very limited.

Ericka Valenzuela, one of three kindergarten teachers, says that the parents themselves built one of the schools, which has only three rooms.

To survive, the *Maclovianos* have hung "diablitos" from the cables near the federal highway to steal power. And they have illegally tapped into the aqueduct that runs under their lands to supply water to their homes.

"We are not shameless; we are working people," says María Luisa Romero, a 61-year-old woman who has lived the last 15 years in the community.

"If we do these things, it's to survive, because the government does not give us any services. As Mexicans, we're entitled to them."

Maclovio Rojas has become a magnet for social activists from all over the world, including the United States. They point to large, multinational companies like Toyota and Hyundai, with nearby plants, and claim they want to control Maclovio's land.

"The foreign activists even see the community in a spiritual way, an example of what Mexico could be," says Michael Schnorr, an art instructor at Southwestern College, who has done social work at the settlement for 12 years. "There's more democracy in Maclovio Rojas than in the rest of Mexico."

To build the schools and social centers, the majority of Maclovio's residents give money or construction materials. The cooperation is voluntary. They also hold community meetings where important decisions are made by those who want to participate.

"The majority of these people are very poor, but at least you have enough land to have a garden, a place where your kids can play," he says.

Digna Reyes is a Salvadoran woman who was deported from California six years ago.

"We're tired of not having basic services the regular way," she said on a recent morning while she washed clothes on the stone washboard of her house made of wood and fiberglass pieces. "We try to survive daily."

Hortensia Hernández, a community leader and one of the original settlers, lives in hiding because there's a warrant ordering her arrest for stealing water.

She denies the charge, alleging that the state government made it up in an effort to dislodge the settlers.

"They won't let us progress," she says.

Even in hiding, she says she has been able to contribute to the community's future plans, among them creating a community market and a sports center with basketball courts and a *futbol* field.

"We have the infrastructure, we have the vision, we have the ambition," she says. "We're going little by little. We don't have much money, but we're doing our projects."

María Luisa Romero, the woman who lives in a tiny house she built herself, says that with the money she makes cleaning homes in nearby housing developments she can afford the basics.

"I'm happy to live in Maclovio Rojas," she says. "It's a community that opened its arms to me when I arrived 15 years ago."

(2007)

Chicano Park Day celebrates a community

Chicano Park is history.

It's culture. It's freedom. Above all, it's freedom.

The thousands of students who recently marched for immigrant rights chose the park as their meeting point.

"Our young people know their history," says Mario Torero, one of the park's original muralists and a member of the Chicano Park Steering Committee, a community group that organizes Chicano Park Day.

"Even if Latino students don't learn about our history in school, they learn it at home and in their communities, from what their parents and their neighbors tell them," Torero says.

The muralist says the park is strong, that it moves people. Besides the immigrant-rights marches, organizations against the war in Iraq and even environmental groups have staged protests there. So when the park's 36th anniversary is celebrated, people also are celebrating its legacy of community independence, a legacy finding new strength in the recent marches, Torero says.

"Chicano Park Day means not only a celebration, but also a liberation," he says.

Founded on April 22, 1970, Chicano Park was the result of a long struggle between Chicano artists and activists and the city of San Diego.

At the turn of the last century, Logan Heights had a sizable Mexican community. After World War II, the city government began to allow the opening of yonkes, or junkyards, and factories that contaminated the environment. In the mid-1960s, the construction of Interstate 5 cut the neighborhood in two, leaving many families without a home.

In the spring of 1970, officials began building a parking lot for the California Highway Patrol on a vacant lot. It was then that residents came together and, along with hundreds of students, seized the land on April 22 and demanded it be turned into a community park.

The activists were looking for a place where residents could learn more about their roots through art.

Now, Chicano Park is home to more than 40 murals and a stage. These murals, painted by different artists at different times, feature Latino icons such as Benito Juarez, César Chávez, Frida Kahlo and the Virgin of Guadalupe. There also are representations of historic events, such as the founding of the Tenochtitlan, the Aztecs' ancient home, and the Mexican Revolution. The celebration this Saturday will feature Aztec dancers, ballet folklorico, music, a lowrider car exhibit and Mexican food – all the color of a Mexican fiesta, says Tommie Camarillo, president of the Chicano Park Steering Committee.

"The feeling you get on Chicano Park Day is that, for that one day, we are all family," she says.

The event will pay tribute to the memories of Marco Anguiano, a San Diego resident who took part in organizing the celebration every year, and Rodolfo "Corky" Gonzales, an activist who was a pillar of the Chicano movement in the late 1960s.

Both men died in the last year.

"Chicano Park is a sacred spot, liberated ground," says Torero. "It's our roots. It belongs to us."

(2006)

Border traffic buck-aroos

Local resident Ernesto Rodríguez used to have two options when he went shopping in San Diego: either buy dollars at a money exchange store near his house or stop at one in San Ysidro.

"Parking, getting out of the car and waiting in line if there were other customers," said the employee of a law firm, "would only take 10 or 15 minutes, but you still don't want to be bothered with it."

Today, it's easier for Rodríguez: While he waits in his car to cross the border at Otay Mesa, the money exchange store comes to him.

"How much do you want to exchange today, boss?" asks Jorge Baltazar, one of the Dollar Boys, who works for a company of the same name and goes car to car to sell or buy dollars.

Rodríguez buys $200, and Baltazar rapidly counts the 10 $20 bills.

"I have to be very careful and give the right amount to clients," says Baltazar, 23.

It's not difficult to spot the Dollar Boys at the border crossing: Their uniform is a fluorescent green vest, hat and pants, and on their chests they display the exchange rate for the day.

In their pockets are the tools of their trade: a small calculator, a pen and a notebook where they record each transaction. And, of course, money.

The concept of a mobile money exchange business was created five years ago by a company called Divimol S. de R.L., in Ciudad Juarez, in the Mexican border state of Chihuahua.

Since the firm began operating in Tijuana last November, the Dollar Boys have become a fixture at the Otay border crossing.

"One year later, the response from people has been surprising," says José Angel García, its manager.

The mobile business – which offers rates competitive with traditional exchange houses – has been so successful that the company is planning to set up shop at other border cities, García says. A branch in Mexicali could open as soon as December.

The Dollar Boys are ready to exchange dollars seven days a week from 6 a.m. to 8 p.m. There are two shifts: morning employees work from 6 a.m. to 2 p.m. and afternoon ones from noon to 8 p.m.

From Monday to Friday, the majority of people using the service are Tijuana residents who work in San Diego, while on weekends, it's used more by tourists or people going shopping in San Diego, García says.

On average, each Dollar Boy serves about 60 vehicles daily, and each transaction lasts about one minute, says Adrián Hernández, a 26-year-old Dollar Boy. The figure goes up to 100 transactions per day on weekends.

"If we take a bit longer, the customers are always hurrying us up. If we do it too fast, we could end up short of money," says Hernández. "It's a lot of pressure."

García says that none of his employees has been robbed because there is a strong police and customs presence at the border crossing. However, the manager says there have been Dollar Boys who have stolen from the company.

The firm's policy is clear: If they're missing money, it will be deducted from the employee's paycheck. If they are short 1,000 pesos (about $100) or more, they are automatically fired.

The average salary for the Dollar Boys is 1,000 pesos per week, which could go up by a bonus of 100 pesos (about $10), if they meet their goals for the week, says García.

Once in a while, a customer will tip a Dollar Boy.

"That's when you make more," says a smiling Hernández.

Manuel Valenzuela, who's been working as a Dollar Boy for five months, says that the most difficult part of his job is dealing with demanding customers.

"Even though the majority is really nice, there's a few that if you take a while to count the money, they hurry you up," says Valenzuela, 25. "I understand them because it's tiring to wait in line."

The service is only available at Otay Mesa. The company has tried to expand to the far busier San Ysidro border crossing but could not get the needed permits from the municipal authorities.

According to García, the vendors who work the lanes at San Ysidro argue that they would lose money if American tourists opted to exchange their leftover pesos for dollars instead of buying ceramics, blankets or other trinkets.

Fidel Carmona, a supervisor of the Dollar Boys at Otay Mesa, says some of his employees have even been threatened by the street vendors.

The company serves customers at the San Ysidro border at a traditional money exchange store that's been open since July near the pedestrian crossing on the Mexican side of the border.

Octavio, a street vendor who sells ceramics at the San Ysidro crossing and who did not want to give his last name, says he would not allow the Dollar Boys to come there if his sales would be affected.

"If people want to buy dollars, that's why there are money exchange stores on the other side of the border. Those 10, 20 pesos they tip me help me to support my family," says Octavio.

Carloo Mauricio Pérez, a spokesman for the municipal department that issues permits to sell at the San Ysidro crossing, said none has been granted since November 2002 because the city is trying to improve the area's image.

Pérez says about 2,500 street vendors work in the area, creating traffic problems and garbage. He said far fewer vendors work at the Otay Mesa crossing, hence they don't face the same restriction as in San Ysidro.

The spokesman stresses that city priorities, and not pressure from the vendors, prompted officials to deny a permit to the Dollar Boys at San Ysidro.

Baltazar says that before he decided to wear the Dollar Boys uniform, he worked at a traditional money exchange store.

"You just sat there and waited for customers to come exchange their money," he says. "Here, you're running back and forth between the cars, breathing in the smog, the sun beating on your face."

On the other hand, it was the freedom of running from car to car that attracted Hernández to the job.
"What I like the most is working outside and not having to be inside a small office."

(2005)

Having some designs on success

It was a recent Sunday afternoon and some 20 Tijuana models – men and women – sported the creations of several of this city's fashion designers.

The runways of the fourth annual Tijuana Fashion Week highlighted the diversity in this field.

There were designs created by young women just learning the trade, as well as those from Ximena Valero, one of the best-known Tijuana designers in the United States.

"This event was a display of new fashion talent," says Rene Tamayo, director of the Tijuana Fashion Week and the ArteModelos model agency. "There are a lot of photographers, makeup artists. We've created a positive energy."

Tijuana is not known for its fashion designers. The industry in this city isn't as developed as in Mexico City, Guadalajara or Monterrey, let alone Milan, Paris or New York.

Yet several fashion shows are held every year, and a good number of independent designers have their own workshops and small boutiques.

"It's a scene that's evolving," says Jorge Sánchez, a 35-year-old designer who's working his way up in the Mexican fashion industry. "When you go to other places and see the professionalism of those events, you realize that Tijuana still has work to do to get to that level."

But Tamayo says the few events that are staged are done to professional and ethical standards. He says he organizes about six shows a year featuring clothes, hairstyles and makeup.

His agency has been preparing young women for modeling careers for almost 20 years. He says that of his agency's 25 most active models, about a dozen work occasionally in Asian countries such as Japan and the Philippines.

"They love the sexy charm of Latinas," he says. "That mix of races, with big, almond-shaped eyes."

For designers, living in a border city is a double-edged sword.

Just like in other parts of the world, high fashion in Tijuana is elitist, because of the high cost of the materials and workmanship. Most residents, who subsist on basic salaries, can't afford these creations.

But Tijuana designers are exposed to both the U.S. and Mexican cultures. The designers tend to borrow the practicality of U.S. fashion, such as easy-to-handle, soft fabrics. But they tend to borrow the vibrant colors from Mexico.

"We have the advantage of combining the two cultures, something that designers in southern Mexico don't really try," Sánchez says.

There's no doubt that stores in San Diego and Tijuana have driven down the price of designer clothing. But living in Tijuana allows designers to show their work in California.

"Why would fashion shoppers come and pay $600 or $700 when they can cross the border and buy a dress at an outlet store for $300?" Valero asks.

To cope with this reality, Sánchez opened Retro Boutique, where he sells his most affordable designs (ranging from $25 for a shirt to $120 for a dress). At his workshop, he caters to customers who can afford his more exclusive creations, which run from $200 to $400.

"The competition in the market is tougher here," says Sanchez, whose professional career goes back 10 years.

Valero doesn't have formal distribution of her designs in Tijuana. North of the border she can charge twice as much: $600 to $1,200 an item. She's looking for a boutique in San Diego to carry her designs.

"It's expensive. That's why it doesn't make sense for me to sell in Tijuana," she says.

In fact, the dearth of opportunities for growth is one of the reasons Valero, 30, decided to leave Tijuana.

She studied fashion in Los Angeles and spent eight years in New York, Los Angeles and Mexico City. About eight months ago, she returned to Tijuana to see her family. She plans to go back to Los Angeles in January.

"I left Tijuana because my dream is to sell my designs in five continents, and you can't do that from here.

"But if your goal is to stand out on a regional basis, you can do it in Tijuana," says Valero, who in April received an award for excellence in evening wear at Miami Fashion Week, an event that attracts the best Latin American designers.

Although Valero has become known across Mexico and abroad, she still participates in regional events.

"But I never forget where I came from," she says. "It's the only time I can take a bow on the catwalk and see my family and friends seated among the public."

And since she returned to Tijuana, Valero has made use of local maquiladora labor.

"Besides being more economical, I help to generate jobs in the city."

She says it's an honor to be able to inspire other local designers who are just starting out.

"It helps to motivate young Tijuana designers," says María Eugenia Martínez, professor and coordinator of the fashion design program at the Universidad de las Californias, the only university that offers such a degree in Tijuana.

Some of her students participated alongside Valero in Tijuana Fashion Week, held last month. The department has graduated about 50 designers since its founding 10 years ago. It has some 60 students enrolled in its bachelor's program.

Martinez says most of the graduates open their own shops.

"They have to start their own business, create their own brand."

And that's how the cycle of Tijuana goes on, with designers hiring models, many of them from Rene Tamayo's agency, to strut down the catwalks at local fashion shows.

"Little by little, the public is getting more interested in local fashion design," Sánchez says. "It's a market that's discovering itself."

(2007)

Tijuana's El Nopal home to arts diversity

El Lugar del Nopal, the cafe, gallery and performance space that has become this city's temple of trova music, turned 15 this year.

"The years passed very quickly," said Adelaida del Real, co-founder of the venue. "I'm surprised how much we've accomplished."

It was 1995 when the space, in the city's downtown district, opened its doors as El Lugar del Nopal, "The Place of the Cactus" in Spanish. Nowadays, most people refer to it simply as El Nopal.

But the space has a history that goes back further.

In the 1980s and early '90s, Tijuana painter and architect Felipe Almada operated the Nopal Centenario. It was a small cafe where patrons could comfortably read a good book, admire artwork or listen to a concert.

Almada died in 1993, and for several months the space remained closed. In 1995, Del Real and Alma Delia Martínez, a journalist and promoter of cultural events, banded together to open El Lugar del Nopal as a successor to another performance space that had been called El Lugar del Juglar, which had occupied three locations previously.

"We started it with very little, but with a lot of hard work," said Del Real. Diverging interests, however, led the partners to go their separate ways. Martínez opened another cultural space, La Escala, in the east side of the city, while Del Real teamed up with her significant other, plastic artist José Pastor, to keep El Nopal going.

In 15 years, the space has hosted rock concerts, plays, movie screenings, performances by experimental artists, poetry readings and more. Nonetheless, one genre caught on and has given its stamp to the place: trova music.

"It was the music I listened to when I was young in Mexico City cafes, and it's what's really clicked here," explained Del Real.

In Mexico, including Tijuana, cultural organizations have relied on government funding, but private donations have emerged as a source in the last few years. El Nopal is an exception because it has always been self-sufficient. In fact, the original venue has grown to include a couple of studios adjacent to the original cafe.

"It's the first independent cultural space in the city that not only has survived but even has grown," said Martínez, who also serves as editor of the cultural weekly *Bitácora*. "I think it offers another alternative for those who have something to share with an audience that's interested in experiencing different things."

In fact, Del Real said that she always ambitioned El Nopal as an alternative to Avenida Revolución.

"We've always tried to make El Nopal a refuge for Tijuana's arts," Del Real said.

In these 15 years, Tijuana has evolved culturally, becoming one of the most important cultural centers in all of Mexico. This year alone, a half a dozen or so independent cultural joints have popped up throughout the city, many of them inspired in part by El Lugar del Nopal.

"I'm very glad that each of these centers has its own identity," Del Real said. "I wish that more would open and that the whole city became infected with culture. Today there's more diversity in the offer, because I see a lot of movement among Tijuana's youth."

Pedro Ochoa, who headed the Centro Cultural Tijuana when El Nopal opened and is now a cultural attaché at the Mexican consulate in San Diego, agrees that El Nopal has nurtured artists and events that, because of their scant commercial content, haven't found a home at official venues like the Centro Cultural or the city's larger cultural spaces.

But this independence comes with a price.

El Nopal survives "literally thanks to the love for art," Del Real said.

The owners worry when attendance drops, because rent, employee wages and their own economic survival are in the balance every day. Profits, when there are any, are pumped back into El Nopal for upkeep and to attract high-caliber artists.

But the work and perseverance have not been in vain.

A visit to the space also means enjoying good wine, a cold beer or a dish with Mediterranean flair.

"I've been coming to El Nopal since it opened," said María Elena Meyer, one of the establishment's most loyal patrons.

"El Nopal gets stronger every day. The sense of community gets stronger. Adelaida and Pastor forge friendships with the customers that are rarely seen elsewhere," she added.

Meyer has participated in several workshops at El Nopal, including a creative writing workshop presented by Tijuana writer Luis Humberto Crosthwaite.

Aside from the many events held at El Nopal, the place has a genuine warmth, due in part to its small size, Pastor said. It has a maximum capacity of 150 people.

"The audience comes to sit close to the performer, not in front of a barrier. It's not the impersonal space of a large concert hall. Here, there is a warmth between the performer and the audience."

This intimacy has prompted Tijuana theater director Hébert Axel González to stage his productions there.

"I know there hasn't been anything as constant as El Nopal," he said. "There were other places, but none that have lasted so many years or that have offered this great variety."

Despite the success, Pastor and Del Real are the first to cite the challenges they have faced in moving the venue forward.

"Aside from the economic matters, the most difficult part has been to encourage the public to take a risk and listen to something they're not familiar with, to get them to lose their fear when quality events are presented," said Del Real, who, along with Pastor, has hosted trova radio shows.

And it sure looks like El Nopal has won the hearts of younger generations. Young trovador Russell Amhir has played there weekly in the past. With him, a new generation of patrons arrived, an audience that was barely in elementary school when El Nopal was founded.

"El Nopal's public is becoming very diverse," Amhir said. "It's a range of people that includes several generations. We can't say that there's only a young audience or an older audience."

For Amhir, being El Nopal's artist-in-residence has meant achieving a professional goal.

"It's a great privilege to play here because it's a very important stage for those of us who play trova."

El Nopal's 15th anniversary is proof that culture in Tijuana goes far beyond painted donkeys and dollar beers.

"It has been something very important, a life project that we've been doing," Del Real said. "We have had economic ups and downs, but we continue with our stubborn character of bringing culture to Tijuana."

(2010)

Chula Vista has a growth industry: Sinaloa-style seafood restaurants

Chula Vista could well be considered the new capital of Sinaloa-style seafood in San Diego County.

In recent years, some 20 restaurants have opened that offer the same quality and flavor as their Tijuana counterparts, and some even belong to chains founded decades ago in the state of Sinaloa.

And the busy season for these restaurants kicked off this week with Ash Wednesday, the beginning of Lent, a time when Mexican Catholics really go for fish and seafood.

In the past, San Diegans had to cross the border to Tijuana to enjoy typical dishes from the Sinaloa coast – characterized by generous use of hot spices and by the freshness of the seafood, especially the shellfish – but a strong demand for this type of restaurants has grown here.

"It was a really good business opportunity," says Eduardo Angulo, manager of Los Arcos, which opened its doors in Chula Vista in June. Its Tijuana location opened some 20 years ago. "The same clientele who used to go to the restaurant in Tijuana asked us to open one in San Diego."

Besides the inconvenience of the long border waits, the violence that has plagued Tijuana in recent months has resulted in fewer people crossing the border to get their ceviche and aguachile fixes.

There's also the stereotype that seafood restaurants in Tijuana are frequented by drug dealers. Some violent incidents last year have further affected the business of these restaurants in Baja California.

In Chula Vista, "almost all the restaurants offer a 100 percent family atmosphere, with a very nice ambience, very calm," says   David Curiel, one of the owners of Karina's, a seafood chain with five locations in the county, including two in Chula Vista.

Practically all the restaurants seek out purveyors who offer the freshest products, and some, like Los Arcos, ship their shrimp directly from the Sinaloa coast.

"The truth, the flavor between what we cook in Chula Vista to what's been done in Tijuana restaurants doesn't change much," said Jaime Martínez, a supervisor at Mariscos Negro Durazo, which opened in Chula Vista in November of 2007.

Enrique Gastélum, manager at Mariscos Hector's, added that, furthermore, in San Diego the quality standards are higher than in Tijuana.

"I think it's not necessary to go all the way over there to find the flavor people want. We have the same quality at similar prices," he said.

Something that differentiates seafood restaurants in Chula Vista to those in Tijuana is that across the border is common for banda sinaloenses to play every weekend. In Chula Vista, on the other hand, is more common to have live mariachis, cumbia bands, or norteño groups.

In Mexico it is known that nothing compares to the Sinaloa style when it comes to seafood. And in San Diego County, la raza knows that Chula Vista has all the flavor from the Sinaloense shores.

But, no matter the place, either in Tijuana or Chula Vista, Sinaloa-style seafood just doesn't taste the same if they're not seasoned with Guacamaya sauce.

(2009)

Hard work won them a place in a diverse culture

Genaro Nonaka remembers the parties at his house when he was a child, parties in which Japanese intermingled with Spanish, where carne asada was served alongside steamed rice.

"The elders spoke Japanese, but us kids used to play around speaking Spanish to each other," says Genaro Nonaka, the 77-year-old son of a Japanese father and a Mexican mother.

He said he's proud to be *Nisei,* a second-generation Japanese living in Tijuana. His father, José Genaro Kingo Nonaka, was a Japanese immigrant who arrived in Tijuana in the early 1920s and became the city's first official photographer.

The Nonaka family was one of 130 families of Japanese origin living in Tijuana in the early 20th century, when thousands of Japanese men immigrated to the southern Mexican states of Oaxaca and Chiapas to work in coffee plantations.

When the field work dried up, many of them migrated again, this time to the north, with the goal of reaching the United States.
Some of them decided to stay in Tijuana, at that time a small border town with a promising economic future.
They began to establish restaurants, open businesses, buy land and, in his father's case, land prominent roles, says Nonaka.

"They were hardworking people who could achieve a lot with a little."

A new documentary by a San Diego filmmaker portrays the life of the Japanese community in Tijuana before and after World War II, a population rarely mentioned in history books.

The forced relocation of Japanese families living in the United States to internment camps after Japan bombed Pearl Harbor is well documented in the United States.

In contrast, the fate of Japanese families in Mexico during this era is virtually unknown. Those living in towns along the northern border and coast also were forced from their homes. It is their story that the documentary "El México más cercano a Japón / The Closest Mexico to Japan" presents.

The film was directed by Shinpei Takeda, himself a Japanese immigrant who moved to the United States 10 years ago to attend college.

"We might learn something from the migration that took place from Japan to Mexico in the early 20th century," says the filmmaker. "When they say that globalization began a few years ago, I think that it has existed since the beginning of the 20th century."

He's co-founder of the international nonprofit agency AJA Project, which helps refugee children in Thailand, Colombia and San Diego tell stories through photography and other media.

The 45-minute film, partially funded by the Trans-Border Institute at the University of San Diego, will be screened during Border Film Week from Tuesday through Friday at the Joan B. Kroc Institute for Peace & Justice.

In the documentary, in Spanish and Japanese with English subtitles, the filmmaker interviews several elder *Niseis.* They share memories of growing up in Tijuana.

Genaro Nonaka offers a detailed portrait of his father, who became a Mexican citizen a few years after he arrived in Baja California.

"He was the bridge between the Japanese community and the Mexicans," he says. "He was involved in everything, very creative, always looking for ways to contribute."

His father was considered the city's official photographer at a time when not many residents even owned a camera. His photos of local leaders, important and ordinary events and his panoramic views chronicle the area's growth from 1924 to 1942.

In addition to the Nonakas, another Japanese family, the Yasuharas, became community leaders.

So Yasuhara, who also immigrated to work in the Mexican fields, was one of the founders in 1911 of the Japanese Association of Tijuana, which at that time organized baseball tournaments and promoted Japanese culture and traditions.

"With hard work, my father was able to open a bar and a restaurant," says 73-year-old Alberto Yasuhara. "Later he acquired more land and opened more businesses. In Tijuana he found a good place to build a family with my mother."

Suddenly, World War II changed everything.

Since Mexico was an ally of the United States, a federal decree ordered that all Japanese, German and Italian citizens be relocated from border and coastal communities to Mexico City and Guadalajara.

Once there, the Japanese were left with nothing, and they had to scramble for jobs and housing on their own, says Catalina Velásquez, who researches Asian communities of Baja California.

"We have to remember that the Mexican government had enormous pressure from the U.S. government to follow its rules," says Velásquez, a professor at the Autonomous University of Baja California.

Most of the Japanese families in Tijuana had just days to move to the Mexico's interior. Others, like the Nonakas and the Yasuharas, obtained permission to remain a few weeks to do legal paperwork to try to protect their homes and businesses.

The families left with the few things they could carry in their luggage and asked their Mexican friends to take care of their properties while they were away.

"They had to sell their material goods at cut rates," says Gabriel Rivera, coordinator of the Tijuana Historical Archive. "It was an injustice what was done to these people."

Some families returned to Tijuana after the war. Others, like José Genaro Kingo Nonaka, never did. He died in Mexico City in 1975, at the age of 86.

"My father was disappointed that in Tijuana there was no support for his family," says Genaro Nonaka, who returned to live in his native Tijuana in 1986.

Those who did return found that their land was now owned by other people and their possessions had vanished.

So Yasuhara, who used to own bars and even a baseball field, was forced to start from scratch. He would never recuperate from his losses.

"They stole everything from him," says his son, Alberto Yasuhara, who lives with a brother and sister at a house that his father was able to keep in downtown Tijuana. The siblings also have a small gift shop next to their house.

Today, about 150 Japanese families live in Tijuana, estimates Nonaka. But since the majority are fourth and fifth generation and many belong to blended families, the true size of this population is unknown.

Tijuana still draws Japanese immigrants, but these days they are more apt to manage local subsidiaries of mega companies such as Sony, Hitachi and Toshiba, which have assembly plants that employ thousands of Mexican workers.

And the boom in anime and manga cartoons and comics also has fanned an interest in Japanese culture.

The Japanese Association of Tijuana, now nearly 100 years old, promotes that culture through community events, food, art courses and festivals. Many Mexican children take Japanese language classes organized by the association, says its president, Horacio Kohakura.

"Japanese-Mexicans are very active," says Velásquez, the researcher. "I think this is proof that this community is having a revival."

(2008)

Urban Corps youth make a difference in Chicano Park

For Alfredo Silva, Chicano Park represents community, family.

"It's a place where my family gets together, for carne asada, for a good time," said Silva, who grew up and lives in Barrio Logan, just a few blocks from the park.

So now that Silva is part of a group of Urban Corps of San Diego County students working on a Chicano Park recreation improvement project, the 21-year-old said it gives him pride to be involved.

"It feels good to help," said Silva, who is working towards his high school diploma at the Urban Corps' charter school. "I feel really excited about helping make these improvements at Chicano Park because I grew up around here."

The improvement project at Chicano Park is funded through a $1.08 million state grant the City of San Diego received. The project broke ground in early May, and since then some 14 students from Urban Corps of San Diego County, a program that gives youth in San Diego an alternative to traditional education through work skills and hands-on training, have been working at the park.

Urban Corps students have installed a new handball court, begun construction of a skate area, and performed demo work on the existing playgrounds. Future improvements include installation of new play equipment, fountain repairs, and landscaping work. The project is to be completed by December.

"Chicano Park is the crown jewel of Barrio Logan and a region-wide attraction for its rich display of art and culture," said Robert Chávez, Chief Executive Officer for Urban Corps. "Just as the mural themselves must be maintained, keeping the park's amenities updated is an important aspect of its preservation. Urban Corps is honored to help provide this deserving neighborhood with much-anticipated recreational improvements for local residents and all visitors to enjoy."

Julio Salas is an Urban Corps student who is working at Chicano Park. He said the Urban Corps program, in which students get paid-work several hours a week, has made a big change in his life.

"It's given me the discipline I needed to focus on my education and on learning new skills," said Salas, who is 19 and is completing high school through Urban Corps. "At the same time, we're helping our community."

For City of San Diego Principal Planner Brian Schoenfisch, the Chicano Park project is very inclusive.

"This project is an example of acknowledging the importance of local voices within the community and showcasing the creative energy of the Urban Corps in a unique partnership with the City," he said. "This is a great way to place youth in positive working roles in the community and show that we can make a difference working together."

Urban Corps has worked hand-in-hand with the Chicano Park Steering Committee and other community members to design the improvement plan, according to Klara T. Arter, Communications and Development manager for Urban Corps.

"I have been watching these Urban Corps students on a daily basis from the very beginning of construction of this project," said Tommie Camarillo, chairperson of the Chicano Park Steering Committee, which manages the park. "I see excitement and pride in their work. The students are now not just working on the project, but they are feeling pride of being part of the community and Chicano Park."

José Casillas, an Urban Corps student who is also learning English, said the program has helped him learned new job skills.

"Now I know how to use construction tools, and I learned how to operate machinery, which will help me get a job when I graduate," Casillas said.

Chávez said that Chicano Park represents a great opportunity for Urban Corps.

"This is a landmark project for us and it's thrilling to see Corpsmembers expand their skill sets by working on a major construction site," he said.

(2015)

No radios on these buses!

Fidel is tuning up his guitar. Just a few feet from the San Ysidro border, Fidel is getting ready for work.

He puts on his sunglasses, fixes his hair, and starts walking towards the bus station.

Then, he starts screaming near a bus door: "Centro! Tercera y Dax! Downtown! Third Street! This bus is already leaving!"

The passengers hurry to get on the bus, trying to get to their destination as soon as possible. Once the driver sees there are enough passengers aboard, he starts driving away.

Fidel jumps on the bus with his guitar by the side.

He goes all the way to the back door and the melody begins.

La Puerta Negra, Cuando era un jovencito, Un día a la vez, Triste Canción de Amor...

Some passengers greet Fidel, while others put their heads on the window and try to go to sleep.

After singing two, three songs, Fidel asks politely: "Ladies and gentlemen, forgive me if I've bothered you with my music, I'm just trying to make a living by bringing a little bit of music to your ears. As you might have noticed, I'm not the best of singers or the best guitar player, but I do it with all my heart. If you find it in your heart to give me a coin, I would greatly appreciate it. God bless you!"

Then he starts walking along the aisle, people handing him coins (one, two pesos, a quarter) and one old lady even hands him a dollar bill.

Fidel thanks the passengers again, and once the bus gets to downtown Tijuana, he starts announcing the streets: "Tercera y Negrete! Tercera y Madero!"

Finally, Fidel gets off the bus, and starts walking towards the next bus across the street.

****

Riding a bus in San Diego is, for the most part, boring. The sign tells it all: "No drinking or eating permitted. No radios or loud music. No fun allowed. Go to sleep." Rarely can you start a friendly conversation with the bus driver. So, riding a bus in San Diego is really lame.

Not so across the border, in Tijuana.

Okay, the buses here have no air conditioner, they're not as modern, and they pollute like hell, but the "feeling" is more interesting than the one you get from riding a bus in San Diego.   Also, it is cheaper: Only 50 cents of a dollar.

True: Riding the bus anywhere is a hassle; it's much better to have your own vehicle than to depend on public transportation. But let's assume you have to ride the bus, I bet you'll like the Tijuana experience much more.

Why? The live music you can enjoy while aboard that funky, old bus.

Probably you're wondering if the busses I'm talking about are some of those provided by local clubs that carry American tourists from the border to Revolución Avenue. Well, no. I'm talking about regular busses regular Tijuana people ride to get to work.

The live music on the bus is provided by musicians, usually guitarists, who instead of playing on a street corner, they play inside the bus.

Usually the songs played by these urban musicians are Norteña and Banda hits, although some do play pop ballads and rock and roll classics in Spanish. There are no official numbers of how many bus singers there are in Tijuana. But on a recent afternoon in the busses that run between the border and Downtown Tijuana, I counted more than 20.

For the most part they are males in their 30s and 40s, like Fidel. But there are also many children, who can be of Indigenous descent, and women.

"Everything we're doing is bringing music to the people while we earn a living with a decent job," said Chuy, a man in his mid-20s that even though was born blind, is a master playing the accordion on Tijuana busses. Wearing a Texana and boots, with dark sunglasses, Chuy told me he usually makes about 100 to 150 pesos on a good day.

Chuy has a partner, Sergio, who helps him get on and off the bus. Both of them make a duo (Sergio is a guitarist) that would make Los Tigres del Norte want to hire them.

Then there's also a man who calls himself Brother Cool, who said he was born in East L.A. but now lives in Tijuana.

"I only play rock and roll classics," he said, with his guitar on hand. "Most of the guys here only play Rancheras, but I have a taste for oldies. I can't complain: I earn a living playing the music I love!"

The bus drivers let the singers aboard the bus because the singers are also "gritadores", or "screamers", where the singer starts screaming that the bus is already leaving and is heading in so and so direction.

"This is a great profession," Fidel said. "I get to meet a lot of people, I get to make people happy with my music, and I get to feed myself and my family. All aboard this old bus."

(2004)

Entijuanarte, a cultural treat for the senses

When Cecilia Ochoa and her business partner, Julio Rodríguez, decided in 2005 to create Entijuanarte, an open-air festival to promote the arts in Tijuana, they knew pulling it off was going to be a challenge.

"It's very difficult to ensure the continuity of independent cultural projects," says Ochoa. "Nothing guarantees the longevity of these projects because they don't have a fixed budget."

Now that Entijuanarte is celebrating its fifth anniversary today through Sunday at the courtyard of the Centro Cultural Tijuana, Ochoa says they have managed to establish a tradition in the city.

"It's a big accomplishment."

If Entijuanarte was a college course, it might as well be called Introduction to Tijuana Art 101.

At least 150 artists will participate this year, and 50,000 visitors are expected. Plus the event features a historic fusing of two musical genres, and one of its presentations will be in San Diego.

Ochoa said that the conditions were already present for a festival of this scope in Tijuana — Baja California is home to several generations of visual artists.

That's why this edition of Entijuanarte celebrates the artistic diversity of the state.

"Entijuanarte legitimizes something that has been said all over the world: Tijuana is a cultural capital," Ochoa said. "When you look at all that people, the families walking among the booths looking at the art made by local artists, you realize that this is not a myth. This is not just a trend. Tijuana is a cultural paradise."

Founded in 2005 by a group of citizens and artists who wanted to change the way Tijuana is perceived, Entijuanarte has become one of the largest cultural events in northwestern Mexico.

The festival has doubled the number of its exhibitions and presentations.

It's a festival with many things going on at once. On one side of the CECUT you might see the works of visual artists at dozens of stands, while on the other side there might be a local rock band or an art workshop for children.

There will also be conferences, dance and performance art presentations, and video projections.

All for free.

And, of course, there will be art for sale, with prices ranging from $25 to $1,000.

"Entijuanarte is a great advance in the border art of our region," Ochoa said.

Artist María Evangelina Rodríguez, who has participated at the festival since its inception, said that the event has allowed her to reach audiences she wouldn't have been able to reach, especially young people:

"There are many families and many students. My goal is not necessarily to sell my work, but for people to learn more about my work, to get them interested."

In five years, the festival has doubled its exhibitions and presentations.

"This festival is the result of Tijuana becoming a cosmopolitan city with a great artistic future," said painter Karen Muro.

To artist Muro, the event "is a taste of the art being made across the border fence."

Ochoa said her goal is for Entijuanarte to become the equivalent of Guanajuato's famous Cervantes Festival in central Mexico.

"Since the beginning we were visionary and very ambitious," she said. "Our region has all the characteristics and resources in terms of talent to make it."

(2007-2009)

Borders commuters pay toll with their health

Thousands of Americans who work or study in San Diego choose to live across the border in the less expensive city of Tijuana. But as these daily commuters spend hours at border crossings, it takes a toll on their physical and mental health. This story was researched and written with a fellowship from the California Endowment and New America Media.

TIJUANA, Mexico -- Fernando Ruiz is getting anxious.

It's almost 6 a.m., and Ruiz has to be at work in half an hour. The way the traffic is moving, he won't make it on time – again.

Ruiz lights up a cigarette, constantly changes radio stations and begins to worry he might lose his job.

He wishes he were at the front of the line of cars.

"I've been in line for almost two hours, and I'm nervous," says the 43-year-old auto mechanic in San Diego. "I've already gotten two warnings for being late to work."

Ruiz is one of thousands of U.S. citizens or permanent legal residents who live in Tijuana, and work or go to school in San Diego County simply because this arrangement is a lot less expensive.

He's one of thousands of commuters that make the daily exodus crossing the border through the two ports of entry in the area –San Ysidro and Otay Mesa. The wait time at the ports averages two hours during peak hours, according to Vince Bond, public affairs officer of U.S. Customs and Border Protection.

Others say the wait can sometimes be four hours.

The economic effects of the border wait times have been well documented: lost hours of workers' productivity, wasted gasoline.

But what is less well documented is the toll it takes on the physical and mental health of the commuters.

Waiting at the border in your car can cause all kinds of pain: neck, wrist hip, knee, foot and back.

And just as serious is the threat to health from inhaling pollutants.

Dr. P.J.E. Quintana, associate professor at the Graduate School of Public Health at San Diego State University, is researching the subject. Her study, "Air Quality Inside Cars Crossing U.S.-Mexico Border," is an attempt to "quantify exposures to toxic air pollutants" by commuters such as Ruiz.

"Exposure to traffic-related air pollution is increasingly being associated with adverse health effects, including asthma, heart disease and even adverse reproductive outcomes," Quintana says. "In-vehicle levels of particulate matter and other pollutants, including carbon monoxide and benzene, can be high in slow or stopped traffic, such as at the ports of entry."

Quintana is working with researchers at the Universidad Autonoma de Baja California to place monitors in participant vehicles to take sample measurements. The study is scheduled to be released later this year.

Exposure to fine particulates can affect lung and heart function in the long run: Quintana says there's an increased risk of heart attack one hour after traffic exposure.

Mayra Ortega is a border commuter who has been dividing her life between both sides of the border for nearly 10 years. She says that after being in line for half an hour, she starts to have trouble breathing.

"I don't know if it's because I hate waiting in line, but I always find it hard to breath at the port of entry," Ortega says.

Tijuana psychologist Lourdes Mariscal, who has many patients who are border commuters, says that waiting in line at the border also creates a lot of frustration.

"That frustration, in turn, creates impotence," Mariscal says, "a feeling of not being in control of your time, a feeling that makes you feel like you're not in charge of your life anymore."

Commuter Luisa Perez is familiar with this feeling of helplessness. "Sometimes, I can't take it anymore," she says. "I feel like screaming in my car.

Clinical psychologist Paul Randolph, who is a governing board member at the San Ysidro School District in San Ysidro, the closest community to the U.S.-Mexico border in San Diego County, says the stress felt by commuters at the border often "carries throughout the day."

Randolph says the stress "affects their job performance, their life at home…. The mental toll is very great."

Francisco Bustos, a 33-year-old English professor at Southwestern College in San Diego County, grew up commuting between Tijuana and San Diego.

As a child, he remembers waking up at 5 a.m. to make it to school on the other side of the border. As an adult, he commuted for nine years so that he could save money to buy a house in San Diego.

Bustos says he was always stressed out, tired of waiting in line at the border. The waits, he says, cut into quality time with his family.

A few months ago, he finally moved his family to San Diego, a decision that has helped his mental well being.

"I feel so relaxed now," says a smiling Bustos. "I'm less stressed now. I have more time for work."

Best of all, he says, "I have more time to be with my family. I can even drive my children to school now."

(2008)

Rafa Saavedra: Writing is like making tacos

I only knew Rafa Saavedra, better known as Rafa Dro, through his writing and a photograph of him I found on the Internet.

The picture I saw matched the way I imagined this writer based on his short stories (are they really short stories?): Saavedra is wearing a Kaliman suit, the popular Mexican comic strip super-hero of the `60's.

You could expect to see a writer with his reading glasses on, smoking a cigarette, in front of a bookcase. But never as Kaliman.

Rafa Saavedra is a writer and cultural critic who happened to be born in Tijuana in 1967. He grew up here, he lives here, he writes here. But don't expect his texts to be full of references to the city.

"I write about my own experiences, but what happened to me could've happened to someone living in Bogota, in New York or Barcelona," he says. "I don't see Tijuana as most people see it, with its immigrants and as the classic border city."

Instead, Saavedra says he hardly makes a distinction between San Diego and Tijuana.

"I mean, it really doesn't hit me when I cross the border," he says. "I didn't even realize they were part of two different countries until I was 15. I thought my passport was only like a ticket, just like when you buy a ticket at the movie theatre."

Saavedra has published two books, "Esto no es una salida" (This isn't an Exit), published by La Espina Dorsal in 1996, and "Buten Smileys," published by Editorial Yoremito in 1996, both Tijuana publishing houses.

One could easily say they are short story collections, but most of his texts don't have the traditional beginning, middle and end one expects in a short story. Saavedra describes his texts as hybrids.

"My texts are not necessarily short stories per se," he says. "I grab anything I want from anywhere. I mix music, TV, fiction and journalism."

Music, especially electronic music, plays an important role in his writing.

"Since I'm also a DJ of electronica, I take `samples' from different sources and mix them in my writing. I play with the rhythm, with music, just like a DJ does. I scratch, make loops."

This concept of incorporating electronica in his writing has as an outcome a soon-to-be-published book titled "Lejos del noise" (Far from Noise).

"When I wrote this book, I would sit in front of the computer with the TV on, with music blasting," Saavedra says. "I would listen to the rhythm and write my own lyrics for that song and add them to my text."

But the intimacy of his own house isn't the only place where he wrote parts of his latest short story (again: are they really short stories?) collection. Can you picture a man reading a book or making notes on a legal pad in the middle of a crowded nightclub, where everybody is dancing and drinking and smoking and screaming?

Guillermo Fadanelli, the godfather of Mexican contemporary trash literature, considers Saavedra's writing a "literature to create addiction."

Saavedra, indeed, is addicted to writing. He is also a prolific writer of brief essays, which are published in different Mexican magazines and Internet sites.

"I write like a taquero," he says. "One taco after the other, one taco after the other, very fast."

(2001)

Mexican comic books, a vanishing breed

Do you remember "Kalimán"? What about "La Familia Burrón"? Or maybe you liked to read "Los agachados" or "Lágrimas y risas."

Even though it was the cradle of some great 20th-century Latin-American comics, the Mexican comic book industry is in crisis, experts say.

During the golden age of Mexican comics, from the 1930s to the 1970s, millions of issues were sold each week. Nowadays, the market is saturated by foreign titles, especially Japanese manga and U.S. superheroes, says Ramón Valdiosera, one of the great artists of the Mexican comic book industry.

Further, semi-pornographic comics have grown popular with many adults, he says.

"This type of publication keeps comics out of the home. And it's also tarnished our work," says Valdiosera, 90, from his arts academy in Mexico City.

The artist — who illustrated some classic Mexican comics like "The Thief of Baghdad" and created the controversial Memín Pinguín postal stamps in 2005 — will speak at Comic-Con International, which runs today through Sunday. (Tickets are sold out.)

On Saturday at 1:30 p.m., Valdiosera will participate in a panel discussion with Mexican-American cartoonist Sergio Aragones.

They will cover, among other subjects, the state of Mexican comic books, which, according to Aragones, are not backed by the major publishing houses.

"There is a lot of young talent creating interesting concepts in comic books, but they do it independently," says Aragonés from his house in Ventura County. "You can find things that are very good, very high quality, but you won't find them in the corner store since they're very underground."

Aragones, a stalwart Comic-Con guest, says he has never seen one of the Mexican publishers, like Mundo Vid, show its comic books at the convention.

"Independent artists come with their portfolios looking for jobs, but Mexican publishers have no presence at the event," says Aragones, an international icon thanks to his work in Mad magazine.

David Glanzer, director of marketing for Comic-Con, says it's important for the organizers to invite authors from diverse cultures.

In the United States, readers of comic books are principally children and teenagers. But Glanzer remembers that during childhood visits with his mother's family in Empalme, Sonora, he would see adults reading comics on the bus.

Juan Manuel Nieto is a Tijuana-based cultural promoter who writes the comic "Los Burrón. Reflejo de muchas familias mexicanas" (Edamex, 2008). He says the decline of Mexican comic books began in the 1980s, when the Japanese manga invasion began with cartoons like "Candy Candy" and "Mazinger Z."

"Children in the 1980s saw only foreign productions on television," says Nieto. "That drove away readers of Mexican comics."

Creators don't have many options, says Eduardo "LaLo" Saavedra, who created "El Burro Gracia," a comic strip whose co-protagonist is one of the famous zebra-donkeys from Avenida Revolución in Tijuana.

"Every day there are fewer opportunities through publishers and the press," says Saavedra, who publishes "El Burro Gracia" every Thursday in Frontera newspaper in Tijuana.

Saavedra, 29, said that although there's less support, the quality of Mexican comics has increased. He added that many Mexican artists publish their work online, often for a select group of readers.

"Mexican comic books, as a genre, as creation, has more diversity than before, maybe even better in technique," he said. "What's almost nonexistent is industry support."

Valdiosera is trying to rescue at least part of the legacy from the Golden Age of Mexican comic books through the creation of the Museo de la Historieta e Ilustración Mexicana (Mexican Comic Book and Illustration Museum), which is in the planning stages.

(2009)

It's rough times for Latino art galleries

Although there appears to be interest in the works of Latino artists from San Diego and Tijuana, the market for Latino art is in crisis on both sides of the border.

Two independent galleries in the region will soon close their doors: Expressions of Mexico in Barrio Logan, and Galeria H&H in Tijuana.

Expressions of Mexico, which concentrated on promoting Mexican art in San Diego, will close Friday due to financial problems and few customers, says gallery owner Carmen Velásquez. It would have celebrated its third anniversary in December.

"I wasn't selling enough to make ends meet," Velásquez said.

More than a business, Expressions of Mexico was "a project to revitalize the barrio with a Mexican spirit," she said.

She reached that goal, in part, and she said the response by the residents of Barrio Logan, most of them of Mexican descent, was always enthusiastic.

"The people from the barrio always supported us a lot by visiting the gallery," Velásquez said. "But I know that the average family in Barrio Logan can't afford to buy original artwork.   Although they wanted to, they didn't have the purchasing power."

She explained she kept the gallery open for as long as she did by investing her savings and part of the profits she makes as a dentist in Tijuana.

Rachael Ortiz, executive director of Barrio Station, a social and educational services agency in Barrio Logan, says the gallery strengthened the identity of Mexicans who live in the area.

"People were very proud of this project," Ortiz says. "If there hadn't been an Expressions of Mexico, it would have been nearly impossible for them to visit an art gallery."

With the closing of Expressions of Mexico, there are only a handful of independent spaces left for Latino art in San Diego.

Ricardo Vela, owner of the Ricardo Vela Gallery that opened this year in North Park, said the problem is that art galleries are no longer a good business, especially if it's Latino art with a focus on the community.

"An idea is one thing, reality is another. Unfortunately, the community complains that there aren't enough spaces for our own, but they don't support them when they exist," he said.

For Vela, the most difficult part of surviving as an independent cultural center is "to create a culture of supporting cultural events, especially those aimed at Latinos and are organized by them or belong to them."

Andy Gonzales, an art promoter and owner of La Onda Latina, an agency dedicated to organizing exhibits of Latino art in spaces like the 24K Gallery in Barrio Logan, agrees there isn't a very strong demand for Latino art in San Diego.

"Unfortunately, there is still the perception among some people that Latino art isn't good enough for galleries and must be sold at a steep discount," says Gonzales. "Since a lot of people in San Diego aren't familiar with our art, it will take time for the market to grow. The market exists, we just have to be more visible and show the talent that's here."

Galeria H&H, one of Tijuana's few professional galleries, will close its doors Dec. 16, four years after being opened by Jens and Petra Herrmann, a German couple who lived in Latin America for 20 years.

Jens Herrmann says they came to Tijuana set on opening a contemporary art gallery after reading in U.S. publications about Tijuana's artistic boom at the beginning of the decade.

But after a few years in Tijuana, the Herrmanns say they came up against a far different reality: There wasn't a strong demand for art. Most of the sales are done informally by the artists themselves.

"Tijuana never developed a market for visual art," Jens Herrmann said. "The artists always sold, and will keep selling, their work, but without a net of commercial galleries serving as a link between the artist and the collector and art lover"

He said San Diego is more sophisticated in terms of its art market, if undervalued.

"To reach the cultural level of San Diego, Tijuana needs many decades. It lacks almost all the elements that a vibrant and dynamic visual arts scene usually has: art galleries, art museums, curators, collectors, art critics."

Petra Herrmann said 90 percent of H&H's clientele came from the United States. In the four years it was open, the gallery sold some 60 works, from small drawings to large paintings. This wasn't enough to cover the gallery's costs. The Herrmanns said they recouped less than 20 percent of their costs. Their prices ranged from $200 for a drawing to $3,500 for a painting by Daniel Ruanova, the artist who's received the most support from the gallery.

"But that isn't the reason we're closing. We're closing because we couldn't create an acceptance of this type of contemporary art among the residents of Tijuana," said Petra Herrmann.

The Herrmanns will keep operating by appointment only until April or May. Then, they'll move the gallery to Cologne, Germany.

(2007)

San Diego artists create art for Ayotzinapa

A group of diverse and multigenerational San Diego artists is raising its voice through art as a tribute and to raise awareness about the disappearance of 43 college students in Iguala, in the Mexican state of Guerrero.

The art exhibition, titled *43* in representation of the 43 students, will be a one-night show on Saturday, December 13th, at Original Gentleman Barbershop and Gallery in Barrio Logan.

The exhibition features 43 works by 43 local artists "in honor and solidarity with Ayotzinapa," the small town in Guerrero where the rural teachers' college the students were enrolled is located.

"The message of all 43 artists is that countless miles away and without borders we are standing in solidarity with town of Ayotzinapa, all the students of Escuela Normal and the families of the 43 missing students," said Elena Marques, one of the show's organizers as well as one of the featured artists.

"Our goal is to take this number, 43, from a statistic to a human tragedy with names and faces in hope of opening the eyes of our community to this horrendous human rights injustice."

Marques said that each of the 43 artists, which include a wide array of voices in San Diego, was given a photo and a name of each student to represent, not necessarily in a portrait format, but in whatever way spoke to them.

"It is important to put a face and a personal story to each of these students because it humanizes the situation, to make it as real and as raw as it is, not only a statistic," she said.

"When these students with 43 names, families and stories become human not a number, it elicits anger, sadness, and a real message that something needs to be done about it regardless of the side of the border you are on. It creates a forum for discussion among artists and the community for a further plan for action in the face of such a blatant and large scale human rights violation."

Marques said that the Ayotzinapa case, which has sparked a wide array of protests throughout Mexico and the world, is similar to the police brutality cases that have prompted protests in the United States.

"It is a universal human rights violation, one in the same with the injustices done to Eric Garner and Mike Brown," said Marques, who is remembering 21-year-old student Everardo Rodriguez Bello with her painting, "The Universal Mother." "It is a consequence of an abuse of power and an overly militarized police force. These students were not wealthy or privileged."

One of San Diego's most prominent Chicana artists and Chicano Park muralists, Carmen Kalo, said that the exhibition is part of the long history of activism present in the artistic community of Barrio Logan and other areas.

"This is a call to action and awareness that the behavior in Mexico and treatment of the poor will not be tolerated," she said. "This art exhibit is an educational format to bring awareness to the public. The border does not stop us from caring; we are Indigenous seeds and these are our relations."

Kalo added that the paintings are a reminder that artists from San Diego will not remain quiet in the face of injustice.

"We stand together in spirits and solidarity with the parents of the 43 students and all those who have been discriminated against in the name of corruption," Kalo said. "We are here to let them know we will not forget their lives the 43 students are worth fighting for."

Another artist, Adriana Galaz, said that people in San Diego, not only artists, should be aware of what is happening in Mexico.

"As artists I believe we have the responsibility to use our talents to create consciousness and empower others," said Galaz, who is remembering student Carlos Lorenzo Hernandez Muñoz. "It matters because the United States, with its unsuccessful War on Drugs, is directly connected to the present day violence in Mexico."

Mexican Consul General in San Diego, Remedios Gomez Arnau, said in an email that the Mexican government "always respects the free expression of ideas" be it through art or through peaceful protests.

But Marques said the Mexican government is much to blame for the violence in Mexico.

"There has been a significant amount of indifference and evasion of answers from the Mexican government surrounding this entire situation and in decades past of human rights violations, which has brought us all across multiple countries to stand and demand answers," she said.

The art exhibition is San Diego artistic community's response –and support—to Ayotzinapa.

"The outpour of support and participation from these artists as well as the community has helped to get our message straight to Ayotzinapa, that San Diego is standing at their side," she said. "The response from us as artists demonstrates a strong, steadfast dedication to human rights."

(2014)

"There is power in art"

One art exhibit remembering and honoring the 43 students who dissapeared from Ayotzinapa, Guerrero, seven months ago is not enough.

That's why a San Diego activist is organizing a second art exhibit titled *43+ Artists for Ayotzinapa*, a one night only exhibition on Saturday, May 2nd, at Border X Brewing, in Barrio Logan, featuring artists from San Diego, Los Angeles, Mexicali, and beyond.

"We are doing a second art show because we have now gone seven months, without evidence, answers, or justice, and are echoing the request of the families to reopen the case and do a proper investigation of the military and federal involvement, and to demand the missing students with life," said organizer Elena Marques, of the Comité Acción Ayotzinapa.

"As a community of artists, we feel art is our loudest voice and our most powerful form of communication to display our solidarity and empathy with the families of the students, to remind the world that this has not been solved, it has not gone away, and it is only getting harder for them, and most importantly of all, to remind the families that they are never, never alone," said Marques, who also organized the first Ayotzipana art exhibit in San Diego back in December.

Blanca Nava is the mother of one of the 43 missing students, Jorge Álvarez Nava. She is part of the caravan that has been taking its message across the United States for several weeks now.

Nava said that events like the San Diego art exhibit give her hope, and strength.

"I'm very glad they're doing this, because it reminds me that there are people out there who care about our children," said Nava via phone from Las Vegas, where she was continuing the caravan. "It's been a very tiring trip, but we do this for our children. We won't give up, and I'm proud to know that there are people who worry about what is happening in Mexico."

The exhibit features the work of more than 43 artists. Marques said that an art piece can sometimes be stronger than a march or a protest.

"There is power in art, and power in a community of artists coming together to speak out with one unified voice. It addresses the complexity of issues that are not always visible at the surface," she said.

Each of the artists received the name of one of the 43 missing students as inspiration for the piece, along with the student's photo and some information about their background and life.

"As an artist, I feel it's a responsibility to take advantage of these opportunities to use our art to voice our opinions, support a cause and bring awareness to local and national social issues and injustices," said participating artist David Varela.

For San Diego artist Mario Chacon, the exhibition is an opportunity to express his outrage at what happened to the 43 students.

"As an educator and one who values the power of knowledge as the great social equalizer, I am aghast that student teachers were targeted for annihilation for expressing their right to dissent," Chacon said. "As an artist who strives to use this sacred gift to humanize, educate, and stimulate critical consciousness I had no hesitation in accepting the invitation to participate in this show. As a father and grandfather of college students I identify with the immense pain suffered by the parents of these heroic individuals whose lives were tragically stolen for no reason."

Diego Yeyo Aguirre Macedo, an artist working out of Mascota, Jalisco, said that the works of art created for this exhibition will be a reminder of the injustice that happened to the students and their families.

"To participate in this art exhibition is important to keep aware of what is happening and not to just put it aside like the government officials of Mexico," he said.

Marques echoed Aguirre Macedo's compromise remembering Ayotzinapa.

(2015)

Danza azteca and protesta define Chicano Park

There are two important aspects about Chicano Park.

There is the cultural part, where danza azteca has been an essential component of the park's history for 40 years.

Then there's the political part, the struggles the Chicano community of San Diego has faced for 45 years since the take over of the land by activists where the park now sits.

Both aspects of the historic site are inseparable, and both will be celebrated on Saturday, April 25th, at the 45th Chicano Park Day, under the theme *El Movimiento Continues: 45 years of Protesta, Cultura, y 40 years of Danza Azteca.*

This year's keynote speaker will be long-time San Diego Chicano activist Herman Baca, who has been an integral part of the park since its founding.

"It is an honor for me to speak, where the Chicano community has gathered for the last 45 years," said Baca, who is director of the Committee on Chicano Rights. "The historical significance of Chicano Park is that it was created out of struggle, sacrifice, a takeover, and the occupation of La Tierra Mia (our land) thru the self-determination of the Chicano community."

The occupation of Chicano Park began in April, 1970, after community activists prevented state and city officials from constructing a California Highway Patrol station in Barrio Logan.

For Baca, the celebration is a remembrance of the many persons, past and present that struggled and have passed, continue the struggle in the movement.

And although much has been accomplished in 45 years, Baca said that, unfortunately, many of the same issues remain. The activist said that in 1970 there were about seven million Chicanos/Latinos, and in the 2010 Census there were 55 million and growing.

"They are the same, and worse than when I became involved in 1968," he said. "Why? Because there are more of us with less of what is necessary to correct the myriad of issues and problems that afflict our people in the U.S."

During the 1970 take-over of Chicano Park, Baca was with MAPA (Mexican-American Political Association).

"I helped politically, and with whatever was needed along with hundreds or thousands of persons from San Diego County, and
other communities throughout California," he said.

Baca is scheduled to speak at 12:15 p.m. at the kiosko.

Just like protesta and political activism have played a major role in Chicano Park history, so has danza azteca for the past 40 years, when danzantes began to meet at the park to establish danza troupes to train the next generation.

Juan Flores, who coordinates danza for Chicano Park Day, said that danza azteca represents the spiritual part of the celebration.

"Danza is our way to connect with our ancestors, with our traditions," he said. "We remember our culture through music, song, worship."

Flores is co-founder of Danza Calpulli Mexhica. He said that danza azteca helps Chicano youth stay focused, and off the streets.

"Danza gives them pride, a sense of culture," he said. "It also gives them discipline, and keeps them out of trouble."

Chicano Park muralist Mario Torero said that he painted a mural in honor of danzante Florencio Yescas.

"He was a friend who I knew when he first arrived in California de Aztlan in the late 60's bringing with him the first time that we were exposed again to our Aztec ancestry though his mastery of Aztec Dancing," Torero said.

(2015)

Church music gets a lift from Spanish view

Christian music in Spanish has come a long way since the days when a single guitar, tambourine or organ was used to accompany church songs.

The market for such music has grown so much and the audience is so diverse that Latino Christian singers cover the stylistic gamut, from ballads, rock and norteñas to merengue and even reggaetón.

Long gone are the hymns that would make you fall asleep during Sunday service.

"People who think Christian music is boring haven't been exposed to the new genres of Christian music that have emerged," says Alejandro Alonso, a singer who is a Spanish-language pastor of Maranatha Chapel in Rancho Bernardo. "Nowadays, you can hear Christian music in practically any style, and it's comparable to the most polished offerings in secular music."

Some artists, after converting to Christianity, have crossed over to Christian music. Examples include Mexican singers Yuri and María del Sol; Ricardo Montaner from Venezuela; and, perhaps the most popular of all, Dominican singer-songwriter Juan Luis Guerra.

Grupero and norteño artists have also recorded a song or two with Christian themes, like José Guadalupe Esparza, the singer for the popular combo Bronco, which had a hit with "El pescador" (The fisherman).

Los Tigres del Norte recorded their classic "Un día a la vez" (One day at a time), a hymn about a man's relationship with God.

Among the best-known, Spanish-language Christian artists are Jaci Velásquez and Marcos Witt, who recently played in Miami for thousands of people.

In response to this explosion in popularity, the Latin Grammys and the Latin Billboard Awards have categories for Christian music.

"Christian music has adapted to secular music," says Ever Girón, producer of Radio Nueva Vida, a Christian format radio station that airs in San Diego on AM 1130. "In English they've always been close, but Latinos are more conservative when it comes to religious music."

Girón says the switch from a traditional style to a more contemporary one began in the late 1980s and early 1990s, when churches launched campaigns to attract more people.

"Before, Christian singers tried to reach Christian audiences. Now, the focus is more on reaching nonbelievers, people who are not close to God," says Girón, who adds that 50 percent of Nueva Vida's programming is devoted to Christian music and the rest to talk shows and special programs.

Christian music in Spanish cuts across denominations. Girón says 40 percent of Nueva Vida's audience is Catholic.

For Dr. Abel Ledezma, pastor of Centro Familiar Cristiano in San Diego, the new forms of Spanish music have given Christianity a new energy, especially when churches must compete with the Internet, television and video games, for the attention of young people.

"It has renewed Christianity. It's a new focus that brings a motivation to get closer to God," Ledezma says. "A lot of churches never thought they'd have those genres, but they realized that to hold on to the new generations, they have to adapt."

Nonetheless, Ledezma says there are traditionalists who don't like the direction that Christian music has taken.

"The critics don't realize that everything has evolved because of technology. We used to read the hymns from a book, then we used a projector to put the words up on a wall, and now we use PowerPoint. We're adjusting to our modern world."

Many churches even have two services: a traditional service, where the hymns are taken from Biblical psalms, and a contemporary service, where the parishioners dance and sing the Gospel to the beat of salsa, norteño or rock.

Alonso, the singer and pastor, recently released a new album, "Cicatrices de amor" (Scars of love, Poiema Records, 2007).

The record is a good example of contemporary Christian music. It has influences from blues and jazz to country rock and a variety of Latin rhythms.

"It's an intimate album with a deep message, designed to lead people to a meditation on the love God has for us," Alonso says.

Like Girón says, even if Christian music borrows from different genres, the mission is always the same.

"To connect with God and the Gospel. The only thing that changes is the rhythm that conveys this message."

(2007)

Conference highlights Latino Christians' influence

One of San Diego County's largest Latino-led Christian churches will host its annual *The Heart Revolution Conference 2015*, from July 12th through the 19th at its main National City campus.

The conference, which includes messages from some of the top U.S. Latino and Latin American Christian pastors and singers, this year focuses on influence: The influence that Christians in general, and Latino Christians in particular, can have on the world.

"As Christians, we are called to be influencers for God. More and more the face of morality is changing and the church is now being asked in a greater way to rise up and respond," said Sergio de la Mora, pastor of Cornerstone Church of San Diego and founder of The Heart Revolution Conference. "[The conference] is our response to raising up believers and leaders who will start a revolution to live, love, and lead, from their heart."

The event features some of the most beloved Latino pastors and Christian singers, including Marcos Witt, who is one of the most known contemporary Spanish-language Christian musicians.

"Every revolution rises up when a person awakens and takes a stand for what's right," said Witt in a statement. "The Heart Revolution is the pinnacle gathering for Next Generation Leaders, Pastors, and Cristianos, to cause a kingdom movement together that will answer the cry of Latinos worldwide! It's more than a conference, it's an experience!"

De la Mora agrees.

"Attendees will leave the conference ignited with a passion to live, love, and lead from their heart while being governed by the values, ethics, and character of the not only the Latino culture but Kingdom culture as well," he said.

The pastor said that instead of religion, Christianity is a personal relationship with Jesus Christ as God and Savior.

"The Heart Revolution is a conglomerate of churches worldwide that join together not because of a religious agenda, but because of a kingdom agenda," De la Mora said. "The unification of the church is the heart of this conference. The more we can look like Heaven on earth now, the more we can bring Heaven to earth for our families and communities."

The conference's messages highlight practical issues relevant to Christians today, including "insights to build a bridge of personal success and spiritual growth for the purpose of helping individuals and families create a strong foundation to win in every area of their lives," De la Mora said.

For Carlos Carrillo, pastor at the Tijuana campus of Cornerstone Church of San Diego, The Heart Revolution is particularly needed in a border region like ours.

"As an international pastor, I have seen the oppression and pain of pastors, leaders, and families, searching for genuine change. The need for a heart revolution is universal," Carrillo said. "Every year this conference doesn't just change lives. It changes generations."

The newly launched network to the Trinity Broadcasting Network (TBN), TBN Salsa, will be on site doing interviews and live recording to bring coverage of the conference and speakers across the world.

Established in 1998, Cornerstone Church of San Diego is a non-denominational, family focused, purpose driven church that is committed to "turn the hearts of youth and families to God and to each other."

With campuses in National City, San Marcos, La Jolla, and Tijuana, and with 6,000 people in weekly attendance, the church has become one of San Diego County's largest Latino-led churches in history.

"Over almost 2 decades, I have seen a resurgence of salvations within second generation Latinos who are hungry for authentic relationship with the God their parents introduced them to," De la Mora said. "They desire to come into genuine relationship with Christ beyond tradition to experience for themselves the fullness of His love, His grace, and His power. The more we give them platforms to meet Him face to face, the more they run to His feet."

(2015)

Jesus is Almighty God
John 1:1

Made in the USA
Charleston, SC
14 September 2016